Rabbit's Pancake Picnic

Tegen Evans **Paula Bowles**

First published 2022 by Nosy Crow Ltd
The Crow's Nest, 14 Baden Place, London SE1 1YW
www.nosycrow.com

ISBN 978 1 83994 110 8 (HB)
ISBN 978 1 83994 111 5 (PB)

Nosy Crow and associated logos are trademark and/or registered trademarks of Nosy Crow Ltd.

Text by Tegen Evans
Text © Nosy Crow Ltd 2022
Illustrations © Paula Bowles 2022

The right of Tegen Evans to be identified as the author of this work and of Paula Bowles to be identified as the illustrator of this work has been asserted.
All rights reserved.

This book is sold subject to the condition that it shall not, by way of trade or otherwise, be lent, hired out or otherwise circulated in any form of binding or cover other than that in which it is published. No part of this publication may be reproduced, stored in a retrieval system, or transmitted in any form or by any means (electronic, mechanical, photocopying, recording or otherwise) without the prior written permission of Nosy Crow Ltd.

A CIP catalogue record for this book is available from the British Library.

Papers used by Nosy Crow are made from wood grown in sustainable forests.
Printed in China

10 9 8 7 6 5 4 3 2 1 (HB)
10 9 8 7 6 5 4 3 2 1 (PB)

For Tom x
T.E.

For Elsie x
P.B.

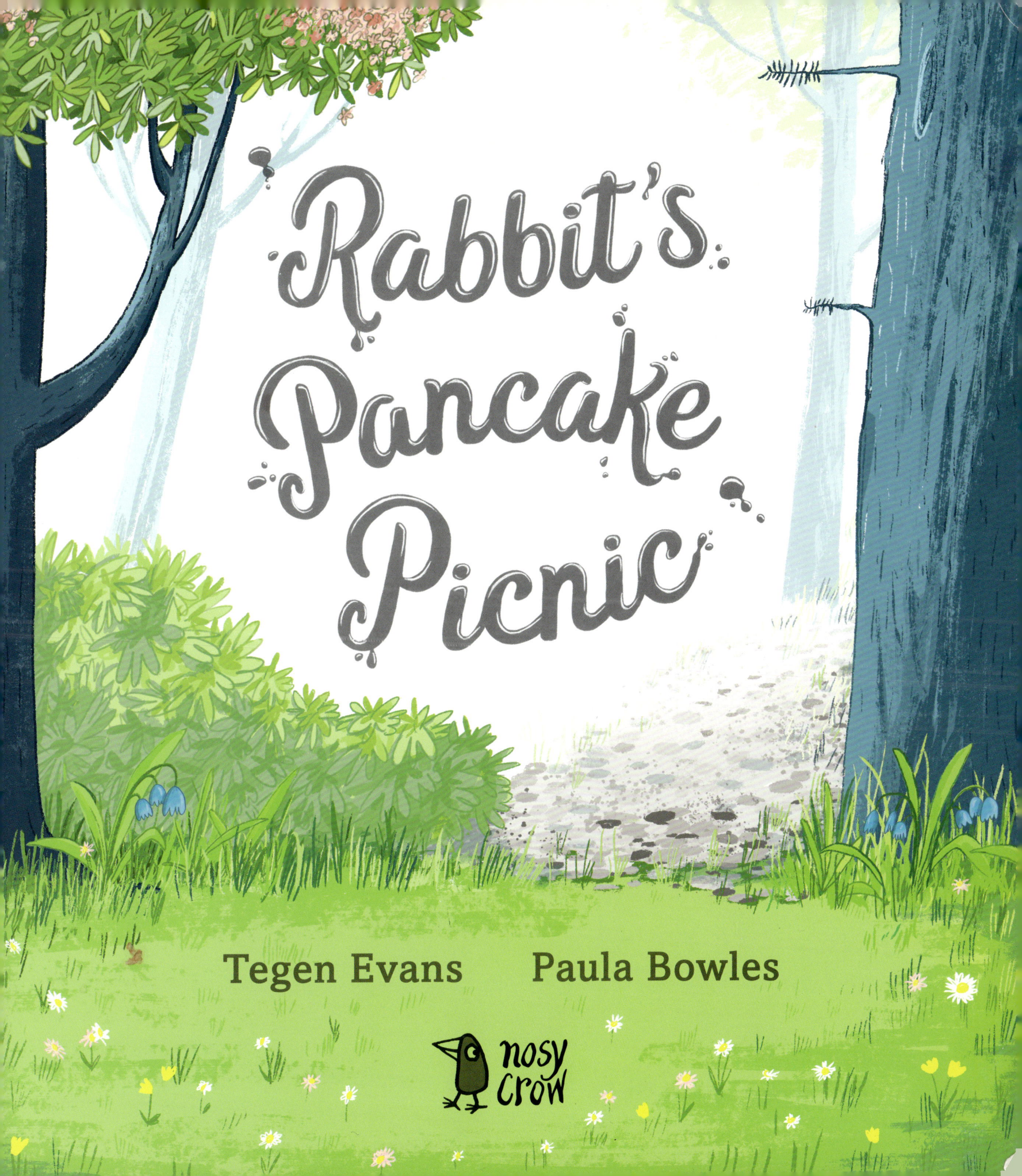

One sunny morning, Rabbit bounced out of bed.
At last! It was the day of her pancake picnic!

She packed her basket with her frying pan, her recipe book and, of course, **lots** of ingredients.

"I won't need **anyone** to help me," she said. "I'm going to make pancakes **all by myself!**"

Then she skipped all the way to the clearing in the wood.

"This is the **perfect** place!" said Rabbit.
"But . . . where's my recipe book?"

She took everything out of her basket, but the book was nowhere to be found.

"Bother!" said Rabbit. "I'll just have to try to **remember** the recipe."

So, into her big mixing bowl went the flour...

SWOOSH!

eggs...

CRACK!

milk . . .

SPLOSH!

"But what comes next?" said Rabbit. "Perhaps I need to add . . .

". . . strawberries!"

And she sprinkled **ten** into the mixture, just as Mouse arrived.

"Hello there, Rabbit!" he said. "That looks a bit . . . **lumpy.** Would you like some help?"

"No, thank you," said Rabbit. "I'm making pancakes **all by myself.**"

But the mixture **did** look lumpy.
"Oh dear!" she said. "Maybe I'll try adding the syrup."

And she poured **nine** big spoonfuls into the bowl.

Just then, Owl flapped down to a branch nearby.

"Hello, Rabbit!" she said. "That looks a bit . . . **sticky**. Would you like some help?"

"No," said Rabbit. "I can make pancakes **all by myself**."

But the mixture was SO sticky, Rabbit could hardly stir it.

"Oh dear, **oh dear!**" said Rabbit.
"Perhaps some apples will make it better."

And she dropped in **eight** shiny apples, just as she heard a voice call . . .

... "Hi, Rabbit!" It was Fox. "That looks a bit ... **strange**," he said. "Would you like some help?"

"**No!**" squeaked Rabbit! "I can make pancakes **all by myself**."

And she threw in ...

seven lemons,

six bananas,

five chunks of cheese,

four tomatoes,

three blobs of cream,

two spoonfuls of sugar,

and one pinch of salt.

But the mixture looked worse than ever.
In fact, it looked . . . **dreadful!**

"It's all **wrong!**" Rabbit cried.
"I've **ruined** my pancake picnic!"

And she ran off into the woods.

"Wait!" called her friends.
"We can help!"

But Rabbit kept running . . .

. . . until she was all by herself.

Just then, Bear bounded by.
"Oh, Rabbit!" she said. "What's wrong?"

"I wanted to make pancakes all by myself," sobbed Rabbit. "But it was a **disaster**."

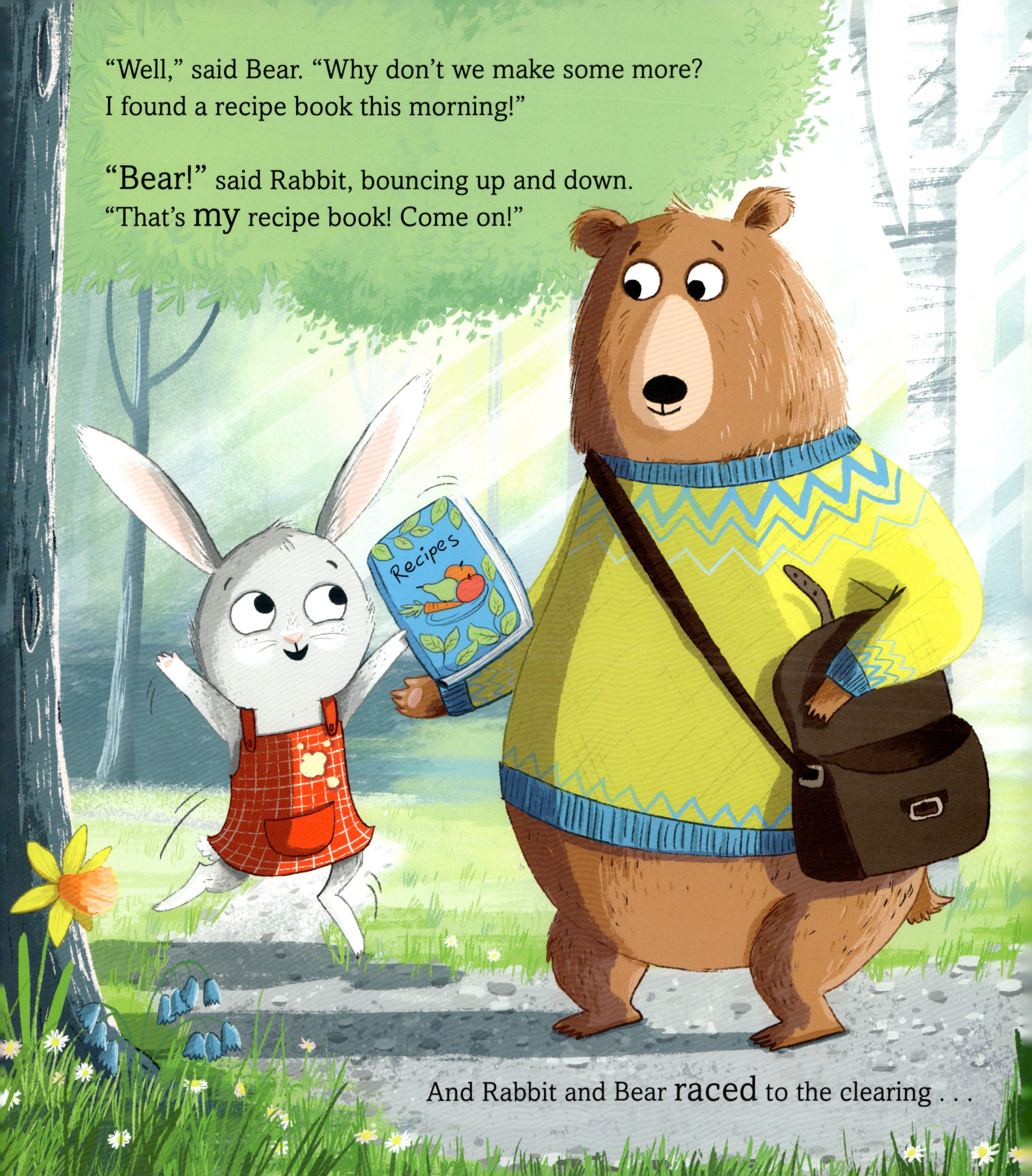

"Well," said Bear. "Why don't we make some more? I found a recipe book this morning!"

"Bear!" said Rabbit, bouncing up and down. "That's **my** recipe book! Come on!"

And Rabbit and Bear raced to the clearing . . .

. . . where all their friends were waiting!

"I'm sorry for running away," said Rabbit. "Let's start again and make the pancakes . . .

TOGETHER!"

"Hooray!" everyone cried.

"We found some extra ingredients!" said Fox.

Rabbit looked at her recipe. "Ah," she said. "I think **this** time, we'll try adding them on **top** of the pancakes . . . **after** they're cooked!"

And so, Mouse added the flour . . .

Owl added the eggs . . .

Fox added the milk . . .

SPLOSH!

And then Bear gave everything a good stir.

Finally, it was time for Rabbit to . . .

. . . FLIP the pancakes up . . .

. . . in swirly, whirly

loopy swoops . . . and she only dropped one.

And, even though Rabbit hadn't made them **all by herself**, the pancakes were **delicious!**

"Thank you for helping me, everyone!" said Rabbit. "This is the BEST pancake picnic ever!"

"There's only one problem," said Bear . . .

. . . "We'll need to make more pancakes!"

Recipe for Rabbit's Perfect Pancakes

Ingredients
- 100g plain flour
- 2 large eggs
- 300ml milk
- Vegetable oil or butter (for greasing)
- Any toppings you like!

Equipment
- Large mixing bowl
- Whisk or wooden spoon
- Frying pan
- Paper towel
- Ladle

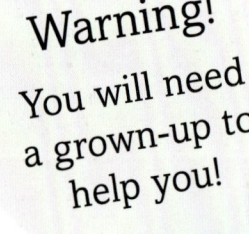

Warning! You will need a grown-up to help you!

1. Pour the flour into the mixing bowl.
2. Make a little dip in the middle of the flour, then crack the eggs into it.
3. Start to whisk or stir the eggs, then slowly pour in the milk until your mixture is smooth.
4. Grease the inside of the frying pan with the oil or butter using a paper towel.
5. Ask a grown-up to heat the pan until it is very hot, then turn down to a medium heat.
6. Pour one ladleful of mixture into the pan, tilting the pan to make a thin and even layer.
7. Ask your grown-up to help you cook the pancake for a minute, and then flip it over and cook on the other side for another minute. Each side should be golden brown.
8. Repeat steps 6–7 to make more pancakes until all the mixture is used up.
9. Add your favourite toppings . . . and then tuck into your yummy pancakes!